Method Acting for the Afterlife

Heather Sullivan

Nixes Mate Books
Allston, Massachusetts

Copyright © 2019 Heather Sullivan

Book design by d'Entremont
Cover photograph from the collection of Lauren Leja

All rights reserved. This book or any portion thereof may not be reproduced or used in any manner whatsoever without the express written permission of the publisher except for the use of brief quotations in a book review or scholarly journal.

ISBN 978-1-949279-11-5

Nixes Mate Books
POBox 1179
Allston, MA 02134
nixesmate.pub/books

For my Hope, Joy and Happiness
Sierra, Rider and Logan

Contents

Jail	1
Magellan	2
Platform	3
Heights	4
Duke Nukem	5
Super	6
Hunger	7
Money	8
Zipporah	9
Game Face	10
Belief	11
Curtains	12
Number Three	13
Lolo	14
United	15
Dragon	16
Lost Connection	18
Rebel	20
Lip Reading	22
Kappa	23
Time Together	24
Barrier	25
Method Acting for the Afterlife	26

Piggy Bank	27
Fighting	28
Lemon	29
Repairs	30
The Dream You Tell Me After the Antibiotic Pump Alarm Sounds	32
For You	34
Grave	35
Fair	37
Gray	39
Safety	41
No Fly Zone	43
Calendar	45
Tree of Life	46
Sailing	47
Seven Years	48
Those Left Behind	50
Cooking for One	51
Night Watch	52
Chordae Tendineae	53

Method Acting for the Afterlife

Jail

When I was seven years old,
I dropped my Donny and Marie Osmond
hand mirror that came with the
matching brush and comb set.
I used to keep my jacks in the lidded box
with their smiling faces on top.
The glass fractured but stayed in place.
I remember my mother telling me that
it would bring me seven years of bad luck.
That's when she enlightened me further
on sidewalk cracks, ladders and spilled salt.
I never knew when a learning moment
might be creeping around the corner.
Open those umbrellas outside.
Shoes off the table.
Death and bad news comes in threes.
I was a Sabbath child made wise
to my seven year prison sentence,
knowing parole would come when
I blew out the candles.

Magellan

You pass through me,
leaving a trail of memories,
echoes of events in the present.
Bread crumbs to find my way,
attempts at understanding the why
behind the what the hell happened
that brought us to the point where
we go through the motions,
watch days measured by gallons
of milk and loaves of bread,
the minimal hours of sleep needed
to ensure I don't drive off the road
while staring at the brake lights
of the truck in front of me.
If I could pick up the pace enough
to catch up to you, walk along-side,
and after asking the questions,
fall back just enough to watch you,
the way your hair will swing,
right arm holding your purse tight,
one foot in front of the other,
but never overtake your lead.

Platform

When I was eight and my brother was six,
a heavy storm uprooted a big oak on the
edge of the property my family was renting.
We could just see our front yard, so it was
still in the field of play. Now horizontal, we
practiced walking back and forth around each
other, the lava everywhere under our feet,
when a stray dog nosed around the corner
of the root bole and let us know we were
no longer welcome. Frozen in place, but
screaming for help, mom came running out
the side door and across the yard, whooping
out "get the hell away from my kids," swinging
the scythe shaped weed whacker my father
used to cut down the high grass out back, the
only weapon we had in the house, as he would
have used any other against her. The dog was
gone in an instant, but mom kept swinging, until
she fell to her knees in front of us, her heart
having moved at a different speed than her
feet, another love lesson ground into my palms.

Heights

We were in the yard raking leaves,
when you noticed a brick red balloon
floating above the trees in the back yard.
Symbolic of nothing and everything
in your childhood and mine,
we broke into a chorus of "99 Luftballons",
making up the German as we went along.
You danced in the driveway, oblivious
to the neighbor boys with their regimented
rules on how to treat the new kid.
I prayed the leaves would never stop falling.

Duke Nukem

When you stayed with my family
during summer breaks from school,
my brother's room was the only place
where we could plug in your computer
On our days off from cleaning the
champagne glass shaped bathtubs,
we would squeeze two folding chairs
in front of the monitor, play Jeopardy
and shareware games we bought for
five dollars in the outlet mall store that
passed for a book store.
Some nights after work, we would drive
to the Burger King in your Pontiac 6000,
sit in the parking lot talking about what
we'd name the kids and having a library
in our one-day house, until they would
shut the mall parking lights down.
Then we'd drive back to my mother's
house, make our bed on the living room
floor from a pile of blankets and afghans,
while the cats walked back and forth
over top of us.

Super

I've longed to have some latent superpower
show up before breakfast, like flight or

telekinesis. In all likelihood, it would probably
manifest as mind numbing flatulence or the

perfect quip 5 minutes after the conversation
ends. The truth is that I already know the deal.

You can break my heart six times sixty ways
from Sunday and I'll still get up for work in the

morning, still make sure the refrigerator is full
and the bills get paid, still put pants on and

wash my hair, still remember trash day. My
power is I keep functioning long after I should.

Hunger

When you are hungry, you don't have the luxury
of being bored, as a gripping sense of ennui will
not fill your belly nor manifest itself into mashed
potatoes and creamed corn.
You will eat once a day at the same time to trick
your metabolism into thinking that's just what
we do now. You can steal ketchup packets from
the dining hall you work in, mix with hot water
from the tap to make budget tomato soup.
You will look through the breakroom fridge,
count the days on the leftovers, watching to see
whether the brown bags shift from their spots
and can be taken home, mold cut off.
You inspect vending machines, looking for hanging
chads that can be nudged down, buy the dented
cans at the grocery store, the marked down fruit
on the rack near the restrooms. Mix it into ramen
noodles for a special treat. Splurge on a cupcake
from the bake case for the baby's birthday,
all the while trying not to think how that could
buy a gallon of milk. You will translate everything
into units of milk and bread, a shirt equals 3 milks
and 1 bread, the light bill equals 20 milks or 36 breads.
And never do the math on the car repair.

Money

Poetry as art, offense,
defense, therapy, explanation,
character assassination, boozy
debauchery, idol worship, words
spewed and spent like endless
currency in the claw machine at
the Buffalo Wild Wings trying to
grab that purple cow in the back
corner that always slips out on the
ascent. We draw our assumptions
close like comfortable afghans
grandmama used to crochet, use
them to warm ourselves in front of
the bonfire made from work we
don't agree with or understand.
Like sitting near the popular girls
table in the lunchroom at junior
high, hoping they'll let us join but
scared of what we'll have to do to stay.

Zipporah

I am a stranger in this even stranger land,
where my words follow a dress code more
rigid than the matching jacket and pants
I hang on the bathroom door every night,
hoping the steam from the shower will
both loosen my nerves and the creases.
I have learned their alien phrases:
in regards to, non-negotiable, week over week.
The women wear pearls and pencil skirts,
carry natty briefcases with other people's
names embossed on them, well-manicured
nails clicking across laptop keyboards
while the PowerPoint presentation moves
forward one achingly slow slide at a time,
no exodus from monotony until the familiarity
bleeds day into day, and all my socks are black.

Game Face

It is falsehood and pretense, wrapped in
a warm green cloak of misogyny, carefully

chosen words dancing on the devil's pinhead,
dribbling over your lower lip and running

down the front of your tie, blooming in a
sepia colored stain on your starched white shirt,

eyes lit from within by the beauty of your
pandering, hopeful my gaze will break, hands

folded neatly in my lap to smooth the hem
of my skirt above crossed ankles. Alas,

you're fucking out of luck today, son.
Wipe your chin.

Belief

Do you have to believe in Bigfoot in order for him
to exist? Can the same be said for Nessie or the

Praying Mantis monster? I need to know how
strong your desire for communion with the hairy

beast of the Pacific Northwest has to be in order
for him to maintain corporal form. Conversely,

if you stopped believing in me, would I fade from
your sight? Would the process start at my feet,

work its way up my thighs, take each arm and then
my trunk, leaving my head and then my eyes for last.

Or would my whole constitution shimmer out at
once, like Scotty beaming me up and away.

We go through our days, in and out of the struggle,
passing by the ghosts of other's memories, the

no longer beloveds and soulmates that we stopped
tracking through the forest, searching for footprints.

Curtains

The distance between birth and death is a series
of curtains, thinner with each layer, passing

through them almost like being birthed again and
again, brocade and heavy at the start, rice paper

and cobweb at the finish. The last one of any
substance held together by your parents, their

fingers interlaced, until what is torn asunder
hastens your progress, and you somersault ass over

tea kettle, ripping through the layers like high school
football players bursting through run out banners

onto the field, the cheerleaders on the side goading
you faster and faster until they are a long forgotten

memory, along with your children's first laugh, your
best friends favorite color, what it felt like to fall in love.

Number Three

I bury my face in the nape of your neck
to breathe in the union of your father and I,
the earthly joy that created this marvelous
human who easily laughs from her belly,
created a verb out of the word chalk,
would blow bubbles on the deck regardless
of the weather, has private conversations
with the cats to discuss world domination
and asks to sample from everyone's plate,
knowing that this realm is a smorgasbord
for her to try, poking her tiny pink tongue
into each bite to test how hot it is first.

Lolo

Stepping out of the shower,
you hop from one foot to the other,
like a sumo in the ring.
Cavorting in naked joy,
hair dripping down your back
making mini puddles on the floor when
you leave the safety of the bathmat.
If you had received the 25 year old me,
I would have already swooped you
up in a towel, fluffing you dry,
but you got me a decade later,
and I would rather watch the water
running down the spine of your
even smaller back, see you smack
your foot hard against the drops on
the floor, the same way you stomp
bubble wrap, push your chair in firmly
against the kitchen table. Your every
move is deliberate, direct. I savor them.

United

Warm bath water bubbles up
between my entwined hands
stretched like a basket in the
middle of my bent knees,
forearms resting on my thighs.
My belly is loose and pouch-like,
forming a tidal basin in the water.
I remember the way my skin felt
tight when I carried each of my babies,
rising up like an island, beads of
moisture running down the sides.
In those still moments, they would
shift and turn within me, the ghost
of a foot or hand making itself known,
until after finding the symmetry
between inside and out
they would calm themselves.

Dragon

Walking through the seaside resort town,
we wandered into one of those new age
stores that I love, filled with crystals,
tabletop statues of Hindu Gods holding
hemp change purses and a back room over
flowing with scarves and outfits that you
can't wear to work. I found a blue tapestry
of dragons circling a yin and yang symbol,
and the intense salesgirl told me they were
longevity dragons. I didn't know if it was
bullshit or not, but I ate that bait hook, line
and sinker standing next to you, shelling out
twenty dollars on a talisman for the living
room wall and a far out hope that I will live
to a ripe old age with all my faculties intact,
and when I go, you'll be a very old woman,
much older than when my mother left me.
Certainly, you can have a good cry when I
shuffle off this mortal coil, but I hope that
your life is so filled with joy and grandchildren
that there's little time to get lost in sadness,
in this stutter step shuffle that I can find no
exit from; I never want this monotony for you.

We used to joke, your nana and I, about how
the Eskimos put their old people on ice floes
when they no longer served a purpose to the
village. Whenever she drove me up a wall, I
would pantomime pushing her out to sea,
the black humor that I was raised on thickened
your skin. She was preparing me for her
departure long before she left. I want to wear
out my welcome, have you rolling your eyes
in the corner, anything to save you from this
emptiness, from the knowledge that I am never
coming back to you, that she is never coming
back to me. I caress those dragons every day,
just like I do the urn that holds her ashes, my
lips barely move when I whisper my plea.

Lost Connection

They finished off my tree today, the huge oak on the side of the house. Eight men in three trucks with a crane and chainsaws, towing a wood chipper to process her start to finish.

Seventy feet up in the air they climbed, cutting sections off that the crane would lift up and over the power lines, like an enormous game of Operation, threading between our house

and the neighbors. She had a lush façade, but was rotted underneath. I was told it was only a matter of time or another intense thunder storm before she would come down, take out

one of our houses or the power lines, disrupt the norm. A massive storm two years previous broke a twenty foot section off, landing exactly in the arms of the three trees behind it. We had

a guy come and remove it before it could work
free for the final descent, crush a car or a child
below. Out our bedroom window, the creaking
as the wind moved in the leaves brought sleep.

When she came to live with us, Mom was happy
to be near the ocean but ached for the woods she
had left behind. After she died, the daily interaction
with her empty spot on the couch overwhelmed me,

so we found this house, the main selling point not
the deck or the tile, but the trees. The huge oak
that I could touch before I got into the car, further
try to connect with everything that I've lost forever.

Rebel

Aside from my last name, my father didn't
give me much of an inheritance.
He parceled out a strong temper, a
profound appreciation of vodka,
the unfailing knowledge that
all crushing love songs were written
for me alone to understand and
a fascination with the motorcycle
in the garage that I wasn't allowed to
touch, my mother's constant refrain of
crushing death always in my ear.
In my thirties, I decided it was time
to get my bike license, check off that box.
Again in my ear, she wondered aloud
about how the children would function
after I had slid under a tractor trailer,
pondered why I loved her so little
to do something so stupid.
I got the license anyway, but
pregnancy postponed my purchase.
Then my mother died. A year later,
I bought a used Honda Rebel from
a little old lady who couldn't ride anymore.

I took it around the block a couple times,
let my kids sit on it in the driveway.
There's no thrill in it anymore,
so it sits in the basement, and I stroke
the seat when I go down to get the laundry.

Lip Reading

I'm not meant for this time or this place.
I know this for certain as I watch their
mouths move in rhythmic patterns that
are supposed to translate into sense and
certainty. Instead, it's like sitting in the
middle of a circle jerk manned by adults
from those Charlie Brown television specials.
I squint my eyes to focus on those pretty
red mouths, but I am Aramaic and Akkadian,
which renders me transparent here.
In another era, I was more substantial.

Kappa

You build me and break me
with your words, oblivious
that I am fractured.
Tomorrow you won't remember
or I'm supposed to forget,
not allow the phrases to tip
the cup of despair balanced
precariously on my head,
sloshing tiny drops over the side,
soaking my collar,
running down my back.
I need to sit stock still,
measure my breathing in order
to keep the water level.

Time Together

There are nights I lie as still in bed as I can,
pillow over my face, arms straight at my side.

In the darkness, I'll open my eyes to notice
how they adjust against the cloth,

take shallow breaths to respect the time
before the air becomes noticeably stale.

It's lonesome with tears hot on my face,
this moment of communion with you.

Barrier

In the dream,
I see the tree coming towards
the window almost as if the car
is motionless in the moment.
Right arm, fist rigid,
arcs towards your seat,
a thin shield.
I turn my face,
both to brace for the impact
and see you, as you were,
as you are,
but the seat is empty.
Sliding through the glass,
I wake before the branch
caresses my cheek.

Method Acting for the Afterlife

The here and now is all part of
your dress rehearsal, our last
chance to get the blocking right,
come in perfectly on every cue.
You have memorized your lines
in front of the bathroom mirror
for what feels like years, trying
to see if your face can convey
the depth of your emotion, until
you realize that this is all so much
method acting for the afterlife.
You will not walk with a limp
unless you put broken glass in
your shoes. You will not die of
a broken heart until you say goodbye.

Piggy Bank

Every happy thought I have ever had
is stored away in a square shaped
piggy bank on my dresser. I dole them
out to pay the toll keeper of existence
like peeled off pesos in that trip south
of the border for low priced pain meds
for my slipped discs that we never took.
When I'm out, I'll be holding up the line
behind me just like when I'd overshoot
the bucket with my change, digging
through the ashtray looking for quarters,
shoving my hand down the side of the
console for the profligate dimes. You
remember that old joke your uncle would
rib any newlywed with, every time you
have sex the first year of your marriage
you put a marble in a jar on the bedside
table, then pull a marble out every time
you have sex thereafter – you'll never
empty the jar. My storehouse is almost
empty, and Joseph, son of Jacob,
has left his post.

Fighting

I force the pads of my hands
against my temples to make
the pressure on both sides
of my skull equal, to pray at
the altar of a second chance,
and in between each breath
feel the way my left lung
catches on my ribcage, hugging
the inside corner like one of
Andy Pettitte's cut fastballs.
I am fighting for my sanity
by the laying on of hands,
calling out *put the mother-
fucking lotion in the basket*.
Harder still with each sunrise
to keep the giggles locked
behind gritted teeth.

Lemon

The last Christmas Eve you lived
with us, before you started your
life with him, we stayed up late
wrapping the children's presents.
You pulled out a bottle of Limoncello,
and we sat there pretending at
being cultured grown-ups. After a
few sips, we came to the collective
agreement that we were better
suited to cheap beer and wine coolers.
The bottle sat in the back of the fridge
until we moved out of that house,
and I poured it down the drain,
the tidy way to spill one out for you,
my homie, my sister, my lemon tree.

Repairs

I would feed you roasted vegetables,
eggplant, beets and squash, tossed
in olive oil, salt and pepper, balsamic
vinegar. The chicken breasts would sauté
in garlic, risotto slowly simmering with
portobello mushrooms and shallots.
Afterwards, a thick slice of chocolate cake
with buttercream frosting for dessert,
before we finish the dishes. Then we
would sit next to each other on the couch,
our stockinged feet up on the coffee table.
You won't have to speak.
We'll settle in like we did when we were
little girls, before we realized how necessary
we were in each other's lives. I would heal
your wounds with breakfast, lunch and
dinner a thousand times over, if it were
possible for food to mend a broken heart.
But far from repair, it'll only provide fuel
for the next sunrise, days of errands and
solitary cleaning, shoveling the sidewalk
alone. When your voice wavers in the living
room and there isn't anybody there to hear

it, does it echo off the wall or just bounce back and forth inside your skull, whipping your amygdala into a frothy hemlock tinged milkshake that you build up a tolerance to over time? Instead of red dye #5, mine has swirls of dead mother and miscarriage. We can sip them with our pinkies out, like the proper girls we are. Maybe one day that sucking sound will be our straws reaching the bottom of the glass and not seeping hope through the holes in our hearts.

The Dream You Tell Me After the Antibiotic Pump Alarm Sounds

You tell me that in your dream,
the one you have night after night,
you are riding a yellow horse that
was yours when you were just shy
of sixteen. His name was Ted,
but you can't remember why.
The sky is perfect and the grass is
a color of green that you can't
quite name. You crest the hill,
just past the place where your
grandfather was born.
You know you're almost home.
You see the outline of the house,
the side yard where your sister
DeeDee should be playing with Mort
and John. Then you see your mother
on the porch, her hair pulled up
in a messy bun. She's waving to you,
right hand on her hip, motioning you
home, but then the scenery starts to
move in reverse, and even though
you and Ted are riding hard, you're

getting farther and farther from her.
And now you start to panic,
you've got to get home,
got to rest the horse,
got to help with the chores,
can almost taste the bread she made
fresh every day. As the house disappears,
the sound of your father's fiddle is
the last thing you hear.

For You

There are no words today.
You're gone from us, from me.
No more beloved nicknames,
deep conversations prefaced
with "now, let me ask you this,"
no more Spanish peanuts in your Pepsi,
the skins floating to the top of the
long necked bottle, no throat clearing
cough followed by that deep sigh
through your front teeth, the way
you rested your left arm over your
right when seated at the kitchen table,
thumb absently rubbing the skin, the
smile that made your eyes disappear.
No more growled "take that" when you
would play the low card, hoping that
I would toss down the higher trump.
Get up on both cheeks, Heddo.
Your heart can break again and again.

Grave

We put you in the ground,
and with my bare hands I
scraped the dirt from the
pile to cover you. With
every rock that bounced
off the box, I apologized for
the interruption, like a kid
tapping on the glass at the
aquarium, my tears mixing
with the cemetery soil,
cementing you in place for
the ages and further away
from me. The preacher, who
theoretically knew you but
spoke in the most generic
of terms, kept trying to tell
us what a joy this was, how
happy we should be that
you were finally home, that
this was just your shell.
But home is over the next
road, in the small three room
house you were born in, the

root cellar with the crazy
turkey that your mother is
waiting to dispatch on the
stump beside the house,
home is on Pennsylvania Ave
with your bride, home is on
my couch with a black cup
of coffee, not this dry, dusty
earth. Sitting at the feet of
the Father is more a chance
for you to keep studying, not
to rest, yet another way to
show that preacher didn't
know you at all.

Fair

An Asian doctor gets dragged from a
plane, while gay Chechen men are
rounded up into concentration camps,
and Syrian orphans hide in the rubble,

as more planes pass overhead.
Meanwhile, the fathers of little boys
with brain bleeds turn to the Internet
to beg for the money to cover their

medical bills in the richest country
on the globe. Today there were births
and deaths, by unseen hands and former
best friends, and today you're gone from

me for a year. It doesn't quite seem fair,
does it? None of it seems fair, because
it isn't. Nothing is fair, and nothing is
right anymore, and maybe it never was

to begin with, because concentration
camps are far from a new idea, and
orphans of war have always looked for
the best hiding places. What I would give

to hear you clear your throat one more
time when I enter the room, suck the air
through your teeth just before you sigh,
to be alive, to still be here.

Gray

I remember when your hair was longer,
and you remember when I wasn't so gray,

my hair or my soul. When we first met I
was sunshine and lollipops, because mom

said a man isn't interested in your problems.
He wants to hear how wonderful he is and

how lucky you are to be with him. When
she'd built up their egos, they always left

for greener pastures. Before my veneer
cracked, it was easier to hide the darkness

from you, but now I'm shabby chic - for
better or for worse, for richer or for poorer

and more likely poorer - like the hutch your
guests say you did such a great job on but

remark later on the way home how it doesn't
match anything else in the house. It's so much

work to set a pretty table, so we eat in front
of the tv and ask the kids about their day.

I flash you when their heads are bowed to
remind you that you've always been partial

to a girl with a dark turn of mind. My eyes
are starting to match the gray in my hair.

Safety

While hemorrhagic fever
decimates villages in Africa,
forbidding mothers from washing
the bodies of the dead,
unarmed teenagers are shot by officers
while open hands plead their case,
little Amish girls abducted from
roadside farm stands while helping
their parents on a day that started
with the promise of dessert
after a hard day's work,
each new learned horror solidifies
my desire to take my children,
bundle them with their favorite blankets,
fill the car with books and clothes,
drive north until we're in the woods
with the mountains at our back
and the ocean in our vision.
We would build a small cabin
and grow our own vegetables,
live amongst the trees.
I would teach them how to fish,
mend their own clothes, sing

by candlelight while chasing fireflies,
their faces flushed with happiness.
And every night I would lock the door,
sit in my rocking chair gazing over
their beautiful sleeping faces
with a shotgun across my lap,
watching for the light on the horizon.

No Fly Zone

My butt was sticking to the crinkly
examination table paper, back
exposed thanks to misaligned ties
on the hospital gown. The doctor
poked at the list, never breaking
the surface tension, until she asked
how often I had sex. I don't, I said,
we don't, correcting course. Her
blinking slowed at my candor.
It was humbling to breathe the
words into existence and watch
them bob round my head like birds
of sadness , the ribbon in their beaks
getting caught in the driver's side door.

I considered daubing the pity from
the corners of her lips with what was
left of my pride, fold it into a pocket
square and then tuck that into my
breast pocket, marked with a scarlet
N for neutered. She dropped the topic,
finding ease in more comfortable motifs
like how everything would be better in

my life if I lost ten pounds and how my
depression over my mother's death
would be greatly deadened by this
prescription she'd be happy to write.
Otherwise, feel free to take as much
Tylenol as you want.

Calendar

It's a delicious thought, unseen demons and long dead ghosts pushing addiction and melancholy. The calendar of time no longer marching forward for them, instead spinning in the corner of the living room like a Deadhead on the mezzanine during a 20 minute jam of Sugar Magnolia forever stuck on a Tuesday. No matter a patch or weekly meetings, the albatross is firmly plastered in place because Great Aunt Martha, who always stuck her bottom lip out when you visited on the holidays, is hanging from the ceiling giving you the evil eye. What's a girl to do, except pull out a TV tray table, line up the Dixie cup shots and ask the old girl to call heads or tails on who goes first.

Tree of Life

I will stand naked in front of you,
strip away the flesh and muscle,
remove each organ and sinew
until there's nothing left but bone.
You'd see the worn cartilage,
the bent lattice and rounded edges.
Can you love the trappings when
the undercarriage is so much
crumbling infrastructure and
potholes, as though the public
works department has been fucking
around, checking their messages
and taking long lunch breaks?
This cage grounds me and I dig
each phalanx into the earth,
rooting until I become something
more for you three thousand years
from now, offering a peach that
will entwine our paths always.

Sailing

Who are the people that go on river cruises
in Europe? Is it the unfunded grown-up version
of Make-a-Wish, where you save up your entire
life to see Budapest from the Danube and hope
your knees will last while you walk streets with
names you can't read or pronounce? You splurged
on Easy Spirit sandals before you left and made
sure your husband had three new shirts. One great
week in your seventies to make up for 40+ years
in customer service shoveling your creativity into
the boiler and watching the next great American
novel swirl up into the sky and laugh its way back
to the first class car. Maybe your fellow travelers
will be 30-somethings who clinched a debt free
start in life thanks to their parent's financial advisor,
like Fitzgerald loaning that ever necessary fiver to
Hemingway. When you return home, you will
spend the rest of your days looking for the right
adjective to describe the sunset you saw from the
deck your last night. That word will finally come
to you, when the warmth from the terminal
morphine drip spreads through your lungs.

Seven Years

She died of an aneurysm in her sleep.
You told me that you woke up next to
her that morning, noticed that she was
far too still, and when she wouldn't
respond, you started CPR, begged her
to answer you, while your daughter,
the last child left at home, the baby,
ran back and forth in the hallway
screaming her mother's name. You
asked the EMT if you had broken any
of her ribs, and he confirmed what you
already knew, said there was nothing
you could have done. She was gone
hours before, claimed by sleep at 52.
During your story, the headache I have
been living with for what seems like
seven years, pushed hard behind my
left eye, and I remembered a scene
from Chicago Hope where Adam Arkin's
character has an aneurysm in the middle
of a convenience store. His headache
wouldn't go away, the world going black
to a pinpoint in the camera's eye.

And now here you sit, offering me another potential way my scene could play out. Until now, I thought it was enough to steer clear of 7-11.

Those Left Behind

At your wake, they dressed you in blue.
Hands folded neatly over your mid-
section, rosary entwined in your fingers.
You looked a lot like the real you, but
your hands were wrong, tiny, almost
shrunken, an after-thought.
There were poster boards on easels
with picture collages of your college days
and reunions, community service. I never
met your partner, but nothing stood out
to me as a reflection on your 25 years
together before her death, perhaps she
was present in the pictures but scattered
about enough to not make a statement
to the mourners, your family's final effort
to sanitize a life they were less than
comfortable with, or maybe they felt there
was a more appropriate time and place for
love. Our image is controlled at the end by
the remaining, mythologized and waxed
poetic, made over into the more perfect
portrait, one safer for their consumption.

Cooking for One

Walking through the grocery store
by myself on a Wednesday afternoon,
the kudzu of sadness is overwhelming
my heart. Little old ladies pass me with
their shopping lists and solitary items,
one tomato, one chicken breast,
a quarter gallon of milk. Watching them
I envision a potential future where the
children are done with me, consumed
by their own families, my husband has
shuffled off his mortal coil and the hottest
ticket in town is the Pricechopper on a
Wednesday at 1pm. They discount the
bruised fruit. These women frighten me
with their ability to buy one can of corn.
To stand alone at my stove and turn
to a table set for one is my darkest fear.

Night Watch

I have looked out on the ocean at night, parked near the large green pavilion at the beach where the bands play during the summer. I have left the car, swinging my legs over the concrete walkway and shifted through the sands, picking up stones to line my pockets. In the dark, the water is an expanse of runway, an undulating field of velvet that beckons me walk forward until the hair circles my face in a weightless dance and raising a seashell to my ear brings silence.

Chordae Tendineae

Each tendon that connects the papillary
muscles to the tricuspid valve and the
mitral valve in the heart can be broken
under extreme stress. Stretched taut
and then snapping one by one through
loss or betrayal, these heart strings,
these tender chords.
Your heart balloons and bottoms out
under the increased weight and loss of
support, just as a suspension bridge
collapses when the cables snap.
Your heart can break in the oddest places,
a doctor's office in Boston when you learn
she will be your last child, on a side street
in Somerville when he says goodbye,
when your mother turns gray in a hospice
room, when your beloved weeps in his
sleep for a dead father.
My heart is suspended in the middle of my
chest by my will to stick around to see who
makes the playoffs. No longer held in place,
she bobs and weaves against my ribs,
looking for the exit signs.

Acknowledgments

Night Watch – originally appeared in *Paper and Ink Literary Zine*
Calendar – originally appeared in *Trailer Park Quarterly*
Rebel – originally appeared in *Lyrical Somerville*
Piggy Bank – originally appeared in *Poet's Corner*

About the Author

Heather Sullivan's first collection, *Waiting for an Answer*, was released from Nixes Mate Books in 2017. Her work has appeared in numerous online and print publications such as, *Chiron Review, Paper and Ink Literary Zine, San Pedro River Review, Trailer Park Quarterly, Common Ground Review, Barbaric Yawp, Big Hammer, Ygdrasil, Free State Review* and *Open Letters Monthly*. She lives in Revere, MA with her husband, Rusty Barnes, co-creator of the three most marvelous humans on the planet, a small herd of cats and the water's edge is just a short walk away.

42° 19' 47.9" N   70° 56' 43.9" W

Nixes Mate is a navigational hazard in Boston Harbor used during the colonial period to gibbet and hang pirates and mutineers.

Nixes Mate Books features small-batch artisanal literature, created by writers who use all 26 letters of the alphabet and then some, honing their craft the time-honored way: one line at a time.

nixesmate.pub/books

www.ingramcontent.com/pod-product-compliance
Lightning Source LLC
Chambersburg PA
CBHW052105110526
44591CB00013B/2354